CELEBRATING JESUS AT HANUKKAH

An 8-Day Devotional

Pyra Lightsword

Celebrating Jesus at Hanukkah Copyright © 2018 by Pyra Lightsword. All Rights Reserved.

All rights reserved. No part of this book may be reproduced in any form or by any electronic or mechanical means including information storage and retrieval systems, without permission in writing from the author. The only exception is by a reviewer, who may quote short excerpts in a review.

Cover designed by Pyra Lightsword

This book is a work of fiction. Names, characters, places, and incidents either are products of the author's imagination or are used fictitiously. Any resemblance to actual persons, living or dead, events, or locales is entirely coincidental.

Printed in the United States of America

First Printing: Oct 2018

ISBN-13 978-1-729133743

Dedicated to all the precious families who sometimes lose their way in the dark night of this world. May Hanukkah ignite your heart this season! Special thanks to my own family for the Hanukkah memories and love.

CONTENTS

The Festival of Lights, an introduction 1
Is it Hanukkah or Chanukkah? 2
History of Hanukkah 3
Why Christians Should Celebrate Hanukkah 5
Preparing for Hanukkah 7
Other Hanukkah Festivities 9
Hanukkah Devotional 11
Hanukkah: Day 1 12
Hanukkah: Day 2 16
Hanukkah: Day 3 20
Hanukkah: Day 4 24
Hanukkah: Day 5 28
Hanukkah: Day 6 32
Hanukkah: Day 7 36
Hanukkah: Day 8 40

THE FESTIVAL OF LIGHTS, AN INTRODUCTION

Hanukkah is celebrated for eight consecutive days, beginning the evening of the 25th of the Hebrew month, Kislev. If using a non-Jewish calendar, you'll want to verify the date as a Jewish "day" begins the evening before the actual day. (For example, if the calendar shows Hanukkah beginning on a Wednesday, then it actually starts on Tuesday night. This is because Genesis 1:5 tells us: "And the evening and the morning were the first day.") It is one of those holidays that does not fall on the same day each year, but it usually occurs a little before Christmas.

Celebrating Hanukkah helps deflate some of the commercialism that Christmas has become. This is because it puts a stronger emphasis back on Jesus, the Light of the World, and serves a strong reminder of His illumination in our lives.

This devotional is a simple guide to help you celebrate Hanukkah. It is by no means the definitive way to celebrate. This book is a culmination of my own research, observations, and Jesus-inspiration. It is the same devotional I put together when my children were young. It's guided our Hanukkah tradition for many years, and I'm pleased to share it with you.

IS IT HANUKKAH OR CHANUKKAH?

My father used to recount the story of studying in the library at school when a student suddenly called out to the librarian from across the room: "Hey, Miss Beale, what's this Cha-nuk-a holiday?"

"Bob, *shhhh!* It's Han-ick-a." In the 1950s, one was expected to be quiet in the library.

"Well, it's not spelled right on the calendar! It looks like Cha-nuk-a!" He got up and took what he was reading to the librarian's big desk. "See the spelling? It starts with a *ch*."

"Bob, *shhhhhh!* It has different spellings."

As a child, this story always made me laugh.

As I grew older, I learned there are actually sixteen different spellings of the word. This is because the word is being translated out of the Hebrew. "Hanukkah" is how the Library of Congress spells the holiday, which is why I've gone with this spelling.

HISTORY OF HANUKKAH

In 175 B.C. the Greek king, Antiochus Epiphanes, ruled both Syria and Judah. In a bid to expand the Seleucid Empire, he forbade the Jews to practice their faith. He also desecrated the temple by requiring that the Hebrew priests sacrifice to Greek gods.

Matityahu haKohen ben Yohanan (also known as Mattathias ben Johanan) was a priest serving in the Temple in Jerusalem at the time. He refused to offer sacrifices any other gods. One of the other priests said he would make the sacrifice, and Matityahu slew him as well as the Syrian official who required the sacrifices.

After this, he and his sons fled into the wilderness for safety. They knew their own lives were now at risk.

He came to be known as "The Maccabean," a title which came from the first letters on his banner—Mi kamochya ba'elim Hashem?—Who is like You, O Lord?

One year later, Matityahu died.

His son Judah led the Maccabean uprising against the Seleucid Empire. After three years of guerrilla warfare, the small, poorly armed Maccabees recaptured Jerusalem, cleansed the temple, and built a new altar.

To rededicate the holy temple in Jerusalem, they lit the menorah, a holy candelabra that was to burn and give light in the Temple throughout the night. Now, the Talmud dictated that only kosher oil could be used in the lamp, but all they only had one flask of oil—enough to last one night. It would take another seven days to prepare more kosher oil.

The menorah stayed lit for the entire eight days—until new oil could be prepared. This is the Hanukkah miracle!

The name, Hanukkah, comes from two Hebrew words: *hanu*, "they rested," and *kah*, "twenty-five." It was on the twenty-fifth day of Kislev when the Maccabees received their victory and rededicated the holy temple.

WHY CHRISTIANS SHOULD CELEBRATE HANUKKAH

Although Hanukkah is a predominately Jewish festival, Christians can (and should) celebrate. It is true that the Lord blessed Abraham because of Abraham's faith. It takes faith to please the Lord. It is said that Abraham's faith "was accounted to him for righteousness" (Galatians 3:6).

Abraham received a blessing from the Lord for his faith.

Faith.

As Abraham's heirs, the Jews are a blessed people because of the promise of God.

Paul, writing in Galatians, tells Christians that they, too, receive the blessing from God through Abraham. Paul shows that the blessings promised to Abraham can also come to Gentiles because of Jesus Christ:

Know ye therefore that they which are of faith, the same are the children of Abraham. And the scripture, foreseeing that God would justify the heathen through faith, preached before the gospel unto Abraham, saying In thee shall all nations be blessed...that the blessing of Abraham might come on the Gentiles through Jesus Christ; that we might receive the promise of the Spirit through faith...and if ye be Christ's, then are ye Abraham's seed, and heirs according to the promise. (Galatians 3:7-8, 14, 29)

Because of the promise the Lord made to Abraham, Christians are heirs according to the promise because of their faith in Jesus Christ. (For more on this, please see Romans 9-13, 16.)

PREPARING FOR HANUKKAH

This book is intended to use as a guide to celebrate Hanukkah. There is no right way or wrong way to do it. This devotional can even serve as a stepping off point to developing your own Hanukkah traditions.

You will need a menorah and candles. A menorah is a candelabra that holds nine candles. You can find these at a Jewish bookstore, gift shop, or online. The candles that fit in most menorahs are kind of like large birthday candles. These can most likely be purchased at the same place you get your menorah. Once you get your candles, freeze them until they are used. Freezing helps prolong the burn time of each candle. (By the eighth night, you will understand.)

One candle is designated as the Shamash candle. Most menorahs have a special holder for this important candle. The Shamash is the candle that is first lit from a fire source such as a lighter or matches. After it has been lit, three blessings are offered to the Lord.

Next, the Shamash is removed from its place and begins lighting the other candles. On the first night, only one other candle is lit. On the second night, two of the other candles are lit, and so on. The day of Hanukkah signifies how many other candles the Shamash will light. The Shamash is the only flame from which the other candles should be lit.

While using the Shamash to light the other candles, Deuteronomy 6:4-5 should be recited as each candle is lit. This serves as a reminder of the greatness of the Lord and of our devotion to Him. As an example, on Day 3 of Hanukkah, as we lit the first candle, we would say the verses from Deuteronomy. We would recite them again as we lit the second candle and again when we lit the third candle. Thus, on Day 3, we'd recited those passages from Deuteronomy three times. (It's a great way to memorize scripture!)

After the candles are lit, use this time for prayers and the reading of the devotional. In our family we also sing "This Little Light of Mine," in keeping with the Festival of Lights theme. This is your opportunity to develop your own rituals and traditions. Maybe you want to pray first or maybe you want to sing first. Do what works best for your family.

Once you finish your devotion, you have two options:
1) Let the candles burn all the way down.
2) Extinguish the candles for use the next night.

We chose the second option when the children were small because we didn't want to risk an accidental fire. We let the children blow out the candles at the end of each family devotional time. To make it a little fun, we had them take turns by blowing on the candles in the reverse order in which they were lit. Then, they both blew out the Shamash together.

OTHER HANUKKAH FESTIVITIES

Some celebrate by giving presents to the children each of the eight nights of Hanukkah. Others have one large celebration on the final night. We have found that celebrating on the eighth night is what works best in our family. That way we all focus on the true meaning of the holiday and save the final day as a celebration that naturally flows into the other festivities of the season.

Again, this booklet serves only as an introduction to this fabulous holiday. More information can be found on the internet or in other books. If you find that you truly enjoy celebrating this holiday, there are other aspects that you may want to adapt as part of your tradition, such as the dreidel game or making latkes.

HANUKKAH DEVOTIONAL

HANUKKAH: DAY 1

Light the Shamash, saying the following:
- ❖ Blessed are you, Lord our God, King of the universe, who has sanctified us with His Spirit. We honor you as we kindle the Hanukkah light.
- ❖ Blessed are you, Lord our God, King of the universe, who has wrought miracles for our forefathers.
- ❖ Blessed are you, Lord our God, King of the universe, who has kept us alive, sustained us, and brought us to this season.

Use the Shamash candle to light each daily candle. As you light each one, recite Deuteronomy 6:4-5:
- ❖ Hear, O Israel: The Lord our God is one Lord: And thou shalt love the Lord thy God with all thine heart, and with all thy soul, and with all thy might.

Thy word is a lamp unto my feet and a light unto my path.
Psalm 119:105

Once there was a family living in a small clearing in the middle of a large forest. There was another small clearing just beyond a patch of thick, tall trees. This is where the family kept their animals in a barn. One winter's night just before dinner, Mother asked her son to go to the barn and get some fresh milk from the cow.

As he cracked open the side door, his mother said, "Son, don't forget to take the lantern."

Now, the boy knew the way to the barn. He reasoned he didn't have to listen because he would be back before darkness settled in between the trees.

Arriving at the barn, he found Bessie's stall door open and the cow standing at the far edge of the corral. "Oh, Bessie!" the boy said, walking over to the old cow.

But when the boy put his hand on Bessie's shoulder to try to lead her back into the barn, she spooked and ran across the corral. As he tried to calm the old cow and move her back into her stall for milking, the light at the edge of the horizon grew fainter.

He finished milking and stepped out of the barn. Taking several steps across the barnyard, he looked around. He looked up. Through the branches of the trees, he couldn't see the stars. Despite knowing his way home, he got off track and soon wandered deep in the forest. Did he get off course as he tried to find his way home? In his mind, he retraced his steps. Soon, his fear and hunger took hold on him, and he started crying. He knew he should have taken the lantern.

"Son? Son, where are you?" The voice came through the trees.

"I'm here, Father!" the boy shouted. "I'm here!"

Very soon his father found him, and wrapping his strong arms around him asked, "Son, why didn't you take the lamp?"

"I thought I knew the way," the boy replied.

Likewise, we think we know our way. But, without the light of the Word of God, we risk getting lost. The Bible is the Light we need in this dark world.

Thy Word have I hid in mine heart, that I might not sin against thee.
Psalm 119:11

HANUKKAH: DAY 2

Light the Shamash, saying the following:
- ❖ Blessed are you, Lord our God, King of the universe, who has sanctified us with His Spirit. We honor you as we kindle the Hanukkah light.
- ❖ Blessed are you, Lord our God, King of the universe, who has wrought miracles for our forefathers.
- ❖ Blessed are you, Lord our God, King of the universe, who has kept us alive, sustained us, and brought us to this season.

Use the Shamash candle to light each daily candle. As you light each one, recite Deuteronomy 6:4-5:
- ❖ Hear, O Israel: The Lord our God is one Lord: And thou shalt love the Lord thy God with all thine heart, and with all thy soul, and with all thy might.

And the angel of the Lord appeared unto him in a flame of fire out of the midst of a bush: and he looked, and, behold, the bush burned with fire, and the bush was not consumed. And Moses said, I will now turn aside, and see this great sight, why the bush is not burnt.
Exodus 3:2-3

The passage of scripture mentioned above is the beginning of the great relationship that developed between God and Moses. The Lord chose Moses to play the leading role in returning His people to the Promised Land, the land of Canaan. Moses, once a tiny baby spared from the hand of the Egyptians, had grown into the man who would lead the Israelites out of the land of Egypt. And how did the Lord introduce himself to Moses? As a flame of fire.

In a barren desert landscape, Moses came upon a strange sight: flames upon a bush. At first it looked like someone had started a fire, but Moses soon saw the flames did not consume the bush. A fire causes wood to turn to ash. Not this fire. Not this bush. The bush was merely a host for the fire. The Lord spoke to Moses out of this bush.

Moving ahead in time we find a group of Christians, gathered together and praying in an upper room. How does the Lord introduce Himself into their lives? The Bible records the event in Acts 2:3-4: "And there appeared unto them cloven tongues like as of fire...and they were all filled with the Holy Ghost, and began to speak with other tongues." Like Moses, the early Christians started their relationship with the Lord with a flash of fire! And, like Moses, these early Christians (and believers today) are called to lead humanity out of the land of sin and darkness by sharing the Light of the Word.

For so hath the Lord commanded us, saying, I have set thee to be a light of the Gentiles, that thou shouldest be for salvation unto the ends of the earth.
Acts 13:47

HANUKKAH: DAY 3

Light the Shamash, saying the following:
- ❖ Blessed are you, Lord our God, King of the universe, who has sanctified us with His Spirit. We honor you as we kindle the Hanukkah light.
- ❖ Blessed are you, Lord our God, King of the universe, who has wrought miracles for our forefathers.
- ❖ Blessed are you, Lord our God, King of the universe, who has kept us alive, sustained us, and brought us to this season.

Use the Shamash candle to light each daily candle. As you light each one, recite Deuteronomy 6:4-5:
- ❖ Hear, O Israel: The Lord our God is one Lord: And thou shalt love the Lord thy God with all thine heart, and with all thy soul, and with all thy might.

———————————

Rejoice not against me, O mine enemy: when I fall, I shall arise; when I sit in darkness, the Lord shall be a light unto me.
Micah 7:8

Being a Christian does not exempt a person from troubles or sorrows. Sometimes our problems are not of our own making. When we are tired and it seems like our problems are multiplying, we must remember our God will never leave us or forsake us. (See Hebrews 13:5.) With our eye firmly fixed on Jesus, He will make the way plain.

However, many times we bring troubles upon ourselves because of our actions or our speech. We have no one to blame but ourselves. Sometimes our actions lead us into sin and darkness. Although we stumble and fall, we have a chance to restore our relationship with God by finding a place of repentance in Christ.

But woe unto the man who thinks he can hide his sins from the Lord. It is better to meet the Lord now with a heart of repentance than in the Day of Judgment. The book of Matthew records a great paradox: "He that findeth his life shall lose it: and he that loseth his life for my sake shall find it" (Matthew 10:39). Another paradox is found in Matthew 21:44: "And whosoever shall fall on this stone shall be broken: but on whomsoever it shall fall, it will grind him to powder." It is okay to come to the Lord as a broken individual. We would not think of trying to make ourselves well before we called the doctor. Why do we think we must get our lives in order before we call on Jesus? We cannot hide from God. We will meet with him, either now or in the last day.

So during this season, take a moment to check your heart. Does it align with the Word of God, or are you doing things that displease the Lord? The Lords mercies are new every morning, and He is a faithful Savior. (See Lamentations 3:23.) Turn to Jesus today and ask Him to be your Guiding Light.

If I say, Surely the darkness shall cover me; even the night shall be light about me. Yea, the darkness hideth not from thee; but the night shineth as the day: the darkness and the light are both alike to thee.
Psalm 139:11-12

HANUKKAH: DAY 4

Light the Shamash, saying the following:
- ❖ Blessed are you, Lord our God, King of the universe, who has sanctified us with His Spirit. We honor you as we kindle the Hanukkah light.
- ❖ Blessed are you, Lord our God, King of the universe, who has wrought miracles for our forefathers.
- ❖ Blessed are you, Lord our God, King of the universe, who has kept us alive, sustained us, and brought us to this season.

Use the Shamash candle to light each daily candle. As you light each one, recite Deuteronomy 6:4-5:
- ❖ Hear, O Israel: The Lord our God is one Lord: And thou shalt love the Lord thy God with all thine heart, and with all thy soul, and with all thy might.

Parable of the Ten Virgins
Matthew 25:1-13

Then shall the kingdom of heaven be likened unto ten virgins, which took their lamps, and went forth to meet the bridegroom.

And five of them were wise, and five were foolish.

They that were foolish took their lamps, and took no oil with them:

But the wise took oil in their vessels with their lamps.

While the bridegroom tarried, they all slumbered and slept.

And at midnight there was a cry made, Behold, the bridegroom cometh; go ye out to meet him.

Then all those virgins arose and trimmed their lamps.

And the foolish said unto the wise, Give us of your oil; for our lamps are gone out.

But the wise answered, saying, Not so; lest there be not enough for us and you: but go ye rather to them that sell, and buy for yourselves.

And while they went to buy, the bridegroom came; and they that were ready went in with him to the marriage: and the door was shut.

Afterward came also the other virgins, saying, Lord, Lord, open to us.

But he answered and said, Verily I say unto you, I know you not.

Watch therefore, for ye know neither the day nor the hour wherein the Son of man cometh.

HANUKKAH: DAY 5

Light the Shamash, saying the following:
- ❖ Blessed are you, Lord our God, King of the universe, who has sanctified us with His Spirit. We honor you as we kindle the Hanukkah light.
- ❖ Blessed are you, Lord our God, King of the universe, who has wrought miracles for our forefathers.
- ❖ Blessed are you, Lord our God, King of the universe, who has kept us alive, sustained us, and brought us to this season.

Use the Shamash candle to light each daily candle. As you light each one, recite Deuteronomy 6:4-5:
- ❖ Hear, O Israel: The Lord our God is one Lord: And thou shalt love the Lord thy God with all thine heart, and with all thy soul, and with all thy might.

———

I am the light of the world: he that followeth me shall not walk in darkness, but shall have the light of life.
John 8:12

Have you ever walked through a darkened maze? Perhaps in a fun house? Slowly, slowly, slowly—you have to work your way through by running your hands along the walls. But, no matter how cautiously you move, it feels as though there is something just in front of you—something you are about to run into. It feels like the darkness is closing in. Your eyes strain, trying to look for a welcome pinpoint of light. Even just a crack of light in the walls of the maze would be comforting.

At the end of the maze, a wash of light floods the tunnel. No faint glow or gray haze prepares you for the brightness. Your steps become sure and your pace quickens. You know where you are going and you can see plainly in front of your face.

Until Jesus comes into our life, we are like that person walking through the darkened maze. We don't know which way to turn. We don't know what is truth and what is only make-believe. Our minds have the power to imagine all sorts of things. Sometimes if feels as if a wall is just inches away, but if you were to wave your hand in that direction, it would slice through empty space.

How to get out? Which way is the exit? Should I go back three steps or move two steps forward?

Life gets like this sometimes. With all the pressures and commitments of daily living, sometimes we lose our way and find ourselves trapped in dark corners, even after trying our best.

This is when turning to the Jesus, the Light of the World is necessary. He is the Light who pushes away darkness. In His light, we can discern the right from the wrong. We can walk with sure steps and get back on track.

I am come a light into the world, that whosoever believeth on me should not abide in darkness.
John 12:46

HANUKKAH: DAY 6

Light the Shamash, saying the following:
- ❖ Blessed are you, Lord our God, King of the universe, who has sanctified us with His Spirit. We honor you as we kindle the Hanukkah light.
- ❖ Blessed are you, Lord our God, King of the universe, who has wrought miracles for our forefathers.
- ❖ Blessed are you, Lord our God, King of the universe, who has kept us alive, sustained us, and brought us to this season.

Use the Shamash candle to light each daily candle. As you light each one, recite Deuteronomy 6:4-5:
- ❖ Hear, O Israel: The Lord our God is one Lord: And thou shalt love the Lord thy God with all thine heart, and with all thy soul, and with all thy might.

———————

Who can find a virtuous woman? For her price is far above rubies....her candle goeth not out by night.
Proverbs 31:10,18

The writer of the book of Proverbs uses the above description to describe the virtuous woman. A long time ago, before light bulbs were ever invented, candles and oil lamps were used to light a house. When the Bible says that her candle does not go out at night, does that mean the virtuous woman kept the flame burning all night? Oil for lamps or wax for candles was valuable and hard to come by. It would have been costly to leave the light burning all night long. Does this mean that the woman wasted these precious commodities just to keep a light going while the family slept? What if something caught fire?

Or does the lit candle represent something else? Psalm 18:28 tells us, "For thou wilt light my candle: the Lord my God will enlighten my darkness." Could the candle represent the light of Christ in our life? Without Jesus in our lives, we walk in the darkness of sin. When we are born again, we are new creatures in Christ. John says that Jesus is "The true Light, which lighteth every man that cometh into the world" (John 1:9). We can keep our "candles" lit continually by having the light of Christ in our lives.

But ye are a chosen generation, a royal priesthood, an holy nation, a peculiar people; that ye should shew forth the praises of him who hath called you out of darkness into his marvelous light.
1 Peter 2:9

HANUKKAH: DAY 7

Light the Shamash, saying the following:
- ❖ Blessed are you, Lord our God, King of the universe, who has sanctified us with His Spirit. We honor you as we kindle the Hanukkah light.
- ❖ Blessed are you, Lord our God, King of the universe, who has wrought miracles for our forefathers.
- ❖ Blessed are you, Lord our God, King of the universe, who has kept us alive, sustained us, and brought us to this season.

Use the Shamash candle to light each daily candle. As you light each one, recite Deuteronomy 6:4-5:
- ❖ Hear, O Israel: The Lord our God is one Lord: And thou shalt love the Lord thy God with all thine heart, and with all thy soul, and with all thy might.

Ye are the light of the world. A city that is set on a hill cannot be hid. Matthew 5:14

I travel about 25,000 road miles each year. That's enough to go around the globe one time, but all of my travel is in America.

All the land, small towns, and beauty never cease to amaze me with each passing mile. Sometimes I stay on the road longer than I should just to see what's around the next bend.

But, sometimes I have to drive late into the night just to get a little further down the road. When I'm tired, these miles seem endless. I watch the lines on the highway and count the mile markers and look forward to the next rest area, truck stop, or town. Many times, my eyes get tired, and I know I should stop and rest. It is dangerous to drive when your eyes are heavy because this is when accidents happen.

Nothing compares with the joy of seeing a faint glow off in the distance. It means rest, a hot meal, or a cup of coffee is just ahead. As I get closer, the vast sea of city lights beckons me to turn off the highway and take rest.

We are all travelers in this world.

And we all get weary at some point.

When feeling like this, it is good to remember the Word of the Lord is that Light that gives the mind and soul rest. As you spend time in the Word, you find rest for your souls. You find peace. "Come unto Me, all ye that labor and are heavy laden, and I will give you rest," Jesus said (Matthew 11:28).

Something about being in the full Light of Truth rejuvenates the soul and gives rest to the tired mind. Being in the Word is refreshment for the soul. Jesus is the Word—"and the Word was made flesh" (John 1:14)—so when we spend time in the word, we spend time with Jesus.

When we carry the light of the gospel in our heart, we become like that city shining its lights out into the night toward others. Therefore, we should not be ashamed of the gospel or afraid to share the story of Jesus with others. Think of all the lost souls—weary travelers—wandering around in the darkness of sin, searching for a glimmer of light, a glimmer of truth. Sometimes our example is the only Jesus these people will ever see. By our words and actions, they will see the transforming power of Christ. Our prayer should be that they find rest for their souls.

Let your light so shine before men, that they may see your good works, and glorify your father, which is in heaven.
Matthew 5:16

HANUKKAH: DAY 8

Light the Shamash, saying the following:
- ❖ Blessed are you, Lord our God, King of the universe, who has sanctified us with His Spirit. We honor you as we kindle the Hanukkah light.
- ❖ Blessed are you, Lord our God, King of the universe, who has wrought miracles for our forefathers.
- ❖ Blessed are you, Lord our God, King of the universe, who has kept us alive, sustained us, and brought us to this season.

Use the Shamash candle to light each daily candle. As you light each one, recite Deuteronomy 6:4-5:
- ❖ Hear, O Israel: The Lord our God is one Lord: And thou shalt love the Lord thy God with all thine heart, and with all thy soul, and with all thy might.

Isaiah 58:6-14

Is this not the fast that I have chosen? To loose the bands of wickedness, to undo the heavy burdens, and to let the oppressed go free, and that ye break every yoke?

Is it not to deal thy bread to the hungry, and that thou bring the poor that are cast out to thy house? When thou seest the naked, that thou cover him; and that thou hide not thyself from thine own flesh?

Then shall thy <u>light</u> break forth as the morning, and thine health shall spring forth speedily: and thy righteousness shall go before thee; the glory of the Lord shall be thy reward.

Then shalt thou call, and the Lord shall answer; thou shalt cry, and he shall say, here am I. If thou take away from the midst of thee the yoke, the putting forth of the finger, and speaking vanity;

And if thou draw out thy soul to the hungry, and satisfy the afflicted soul; **then shall thy <u>light</u> rise in obscurity, and thy darkness be as the noon day:**

And the Lord shall guide thee continually, and satisfy thy soul in drought, and make fat thy bones: and thou shalt be like a watered garden, and like a spring of water, whose waters fail not.

And they that shall be of thee shall build the old waste places: thou shalt raise up the foundations of many generations; and thou shalt be called, The repairer of the breach, The restorer of paths to dwell in.

If thou turn away thy foot from the sabbath, from doing thy pleasure on my holy day; and call the sabbath a delight, the holy of the Lord, honorable; and shalt honor him, not doing thine own ways, nor finding thine own pleasure, nor speaking thine own words:

Then shalt thou delight thyself in the Lord; and I will cause thee to ride upon the high places of the earth, and feed thee with the heritage of Jacob thy father; for the mouth of the Lord hath spoken it.

Made in the USA
San Bernardino, CA
11 December 2019